ISBN: 9798389549449

THE MELTING POT

A Mental Health Anthology

Episode 3

Table of Contents

Introduction

If you are perpetually wearing rose-tinted spectacles, the wor looks great, but the view is not usually real. The original idea The Melting Pot, this series of poetry anthologies written people who have things they want to get off their chests, due their brushes with mental health problems, was very exciting prospect. It was something that one might expect people to hav put energy into for both emotional and creative reason simultaneously. As a long-term schizophrenic and also a write decided to give it a try as a project. I figured nobody else w better placed.

Knowing the extent of widespread and increasing troubles of th nature, around a large proportion of the world, to curate th project over the internet was an exciting thought. The optimis that built quickly was encouraging; momentum rose, and lo ar behold, it wasn't very long before 'The Melting Pot Episode 1 - Mental Health Anthology' was published. The date of publicatio was 26 November 2022, a month before Christmas, and arou the Facebook Group through which I co-ordinated things the was a detectable buzz of anticipation. I spread the wo everywhere I could think of; and many people in the group mad noises about how and where to promote it.

Alarm bells rang fairly soon. The membership of the Grou originally rocketing to the heavens in number, up to over 400 the space of a few weeks, stopped increasing. Submissions poetry, which had also been meteoric in climbing to lar amounts, also reached a plateau. For a while, a reliable core keen contributors carried on creating pieces, and nobody el

8

as doing anything. I continued pursuing it and it turned out to
e no more than a temporary blip. Here we are at Episode 3.

eas about what to do to make the project known to a wider
llowing, have been in steady motion. I contacted the mental
ealth charity MIND more than a dozen times, expecting keen
utual interest, but they initially ignored me completely - apart
om one invitation to write a blog post, which I dropped all my
her work to create in less than 24 hours. But when I returned it
 them I heard nothing more about it. I had asked for a contact
ame to liaise with, and they ignored that as well. Fortunately,
th much dogged persistence on my part, they and I began to
mmunicate, and there has now been helpful dialogue and
llaboration. Rather than be seen to 'promote' The Melting Pot
elf they asked me to write more of an autobiographical piece;
t in the end, one hopes that my long-term mental health
oblems help show the relevance and significance of the project
 the wider sphere.

ne MIND Boggles' poem is something I wrote about the
stration at being ignored, and there are some angry
dertones to it (though it has been edited); perhaps it somehow
ached out into the ether and magically manifested the
nstructive interactions that followed. All's well that ends well!

 add insult to injury, there is the not-insignificant topic of the
aded, and much-discussed, Facebook algorithms. In years
st it was easy to connect with friends and followers about, for
ample, a poetry anthology project (!) catering for a specialised
mographic or sector. You could put up a post on a personal
file page, or other page, and substantial numbers would see
and so forth. Nowadays, the reach has been heavily doctored;
ngs have been deliberately limited to much, much smaller

audiences and visibility. Every user knows of it and we have
been adversely affected by it. The reason most spoken of, is th
Facebook wanted to make more use of - and revenue from
advertising. That sounds feasible and likely. It was a shift from
personal website experience to a commercial one, and as far
The Melting Pot is concerned it has been a hindrance to effect
propagation. A factor which is making further 'Episodes' mo
difficult to put together. Yet so far, we have been able to contin
and have the momentum to keep the project active and alive.

The development of a website for my own books is in progre
I write every day in parallel to this work. I have three other boo
of my own progressing within a busy writing pipeline.

Episode 3 is a longer book than 1 and 2, meaning a sligh
higher printing cost and (therefore) retail price.

My heartfelt thanks go out to everyone that has seen the val
of this series, and to the poets and contributors. Melting Pot 3
now with us; poems and new members continue to come in; a
although the workload is considerable, the benefits to mer
health are immeasurably greater. We have reason to be prou

Submissions remain open.

Stuart Watkins
Curator, The Melting Pot 3, April 2023.

The Pot's Poets

Amita Sarjit Ahluwalia

.....is one of the pen names of multilingual Indian poet Amita Paul, who writes sensitively on a wide range of subjects, including the human mind.

Jane Badrock

Jane Badrock's career, for many a year,
was in Finance, until she called time.
She painted, she read, now writes fiction instead,
and sometimes, ridiculous rhyme.

Tasha Bennett

Tasha is a trauma-informed psychotherapist based in Greater Manchester, UK, working with sandplay therapy, sound healing, Pesso Boyden therapy, art and poetry.

Jo Broderick

Jo is 33 years old and from Weston-super-Mare. She suffers with depression, anxiety and type 1 diabetes. She has been writing since she was 15.

Anne Buchanan-Brown

Anne is a former English teacher, mother, grandmother, and pagan. She has lived with depression for decades, but still likes to laugh.

11

Teresa Bullock (Marcano)

Teresa is a nurse by profession and a poet at heart. When her mind is taken hostage by this world, she reaches for her pen and releases her soul.

Isabelle P Byrne

Isabelle is a 29-year-old female poet from Manchester. Her work focuses upon her experiences of hospitalisation, electro convulsive therapy and navigating recovery with a "ruined" identity.

Catherine Campbell

Catherine lives in Papamoa, New Zealand. She has experienced both post-natal and physiological depression, and has always found writing a source of comfort, joy, and transformation.

Colleen Cavell

Colleen came to writing late….lives with a cat….and writes from the heart quickly with little editing. She tries to keep out of boxes and stay in the now.

Douglas Colston

Douglas (53 years old and from Australia's Sunshine Coast) has heaps of life experience and consequently - in part - he deals with mental and physical illnesses daily, in addition to writing.

Susan ILA Davis

Susan is from Michigan. She wrote her first poem at 11. She shares empathy with words, tucked between the pages like pressed flowers and sketches of years gone. Head held high, she survived.

Rose Drew

Rose is a performance poet, publisher, teacher, and anthropologist. She's worked her way through PTSD, anorexia and learned to love her mild autism. Rose is tall on the inside.
www.yorkspokenword.org.uk

Grace Fry-Rannila

Grace is a queer, punk rock writer living in southern Oklahoma. Her writing focuses on issues such as mental health and personal sovereignty.

Ian Hall

Ian is a published performance poet of over 50 years' experience. He is also a film-maker, collaborator, publisher, facilitator, producer, host and a profoundly deaf taxi driver.

John Highton

John is a 41-year-old builder, from Oldham. He suffers with ADHD and PTSD, and has been writing for 26 years. Poetry is the way he releases his abstract thoughts and feelings.

Maura Hogan

Maura is from Massachusetts. She finds writing poetry organi
and soothing. From a family of word lovers, Maura says that
poetry helps her express her rich inner thoughts and feelings

Sarah Jane Hull

Sarah lives in Kent. Growing up in a household affected by
mental health, domestic violence, and alcohol abuse, she
writes about issues to make sense of her past.

Tabbie Hunt

Tabbie is a book-packager turned freelance writer. She write:
when the daily grind lets up, and has had short fiction publish
by Daily Science Fiction and Gingerbread House, among
others.

Chris Husband

Chris, an author from Lancashire, has written poems for as l
as he can remember and is a published poet of two collectio
- "Chips for Teal" and "Food for Thought".

Charlene Ima-Obong Efiong

Charlene is 14 years old and from Nigeria. She is currently a
college at ENLIS and aspires to be a writer in the future.

Paul Lepper

Paul, aka 'Pablo Rouge', is a 34-year-old actor and poet originally from South London, now living in North London with his partner of 7 years.

Laura Mochan

Laura is 46 years young; mother of one beautiful boy, lover of words and music, writer, editor, charity worker, master procrastinator and an eternal student.

Ille Mort

Ille is a Wyrd-Woman and atypical poet who lives with C-TSD. Her work explores both dark and light, also the liminal twilight lurking between them.

Robert Phillips

Robert is 59 years old and an ex-lorry driver from Kirkby, Liverpool. He is married with three children and has suffered with depression for years; he says that poetry has been his salvation.

Mahona Pita

Mahona is from New Zealand. He is a happily married, retired grandfather. Poetry is his passion and refuge, enabling escape from a world seemingly hell bent on conformity.

Matt Pugh

Matt is a Welsh Valley's man, proud Dad to three wonderful daughters. He rediscovered writing in his 40's and loves poem and stories for their catharsis.

Elaine Samuels

Elaine, a singer/songwriter/guitarist, gigging solo and with her Kindred Spirit Band, has featured on television, radio, Glastonbury and clubs and festivals throughout the UK.

Peter Sanderson

Peter is 61 years of age, from Glasgow but living in Suffolk. H partner and daughter both have mental health problems. They are his inspiration.

Sunil Sharma

Dr. Sunil Sharma, ophthalmologist, writes poems and articles Hindi and English, regularly published in local newspapers an monthlies. He has had two Hindi poetry collections and five joint collections published.

Dorn Simon

Dorn is 55 (writing poetry for 48!), a pro-published writer/film producer. Diagnosed at 30 with bipolar-II, BPD, OCD, ADHD, and C-PTSD. She was born in Colchester and now lives in Ireland.

aema Sinclair

aema hails from Glastonbury. Darkness and light collide. Poet nd adventurer.

ason N Smith

ason is an awarded writer and spoken word artist, who has ad at the Roundhouse, Royal Festival Hall, Tate Modern, ational Theatre, and The St. Ethelburga's Centre for econciliation and Peace.

ee Smith

his 62-year-old, singing AI man turned to poetry seven years go, publishing last year. He writes of events and life xperiences through rhyming couplets.

hristine Smuniewski

hristine is a 30-year-old poet in Tennessee, United States. oetry gets her through both her best and darkest days. Her achshund is the center of her world.

ae Stenson

ae, a late bloomer, gained an English degree at 38 and a eative Writing MA at 57. Currently, she is working on her first vel, focusing on society's outsiders.

Janet Tai

Janet is aged 62 and from Malaysia. She has been writing since the early eighties. She was diagnosed with dysthymia (doubled depression) in 2018.

Gwen Taylor

Gwen is a British poetess/songstress. She has been diagnos with paranoid schizophrenia and psychosis. A caring person, her aim is to keep everybody alive, safe, happy and well.

John Thornton

John is an immigrant's son.

Trudy Annie

Trudy says………one life, one dream, keep it real…..in a wo where you can be anyone, be yourself. To know yourself is important. She loves poetry and writing; always has and alwa will.

Ariuna Turi

Ariuna is a 25-year-old Brazilian living in America, trying to fi his place in life and the world.

Yvonne Ugarte

Yvonne is a performance poet and songwriter from Leeds. She has been writing since she was 5 years old and just had her second book 'My Aunt Jean's a Dinosaur' published.

Carol Ward

Carol is a writer and poet from Kent. She experiences mental health issues as well as supports those who do.

Philippa Waters

Philippa is 62, from Hampshire. She has clinical depression, anxiety and agoraphobia. She has always written but started seriously in 2004. She writes poetry and prose.

Stuart Watkins

Schizophrenic, since 1994. Author: 'A United Kingdom' - Trains of Logical Thought (2019), Cosmic Visions (2021), The Ocean (2021), Cataclysmic Vibrations (2022).
Curator: Pandemic Poets (2022), The Melting Pot (2022/3).

Paul Wilkins

Paul is a very witty poet
And now you've come to know it
He also has a G.S.O.H.
And that's not just a rumour

Elmien Wolvaardt

Elmien is York's only Afrikaans poet. Her sparse, yet resonant poems reflect on - and occasionally rebel against - the gentle and not-so-gentle oppressions of life, love and motherhood.

Sacred Space

Anne Buchanan-Brown

Treading in soft-socked laughter,
These women
Carry love and acceptance
Up the stairs
From the kitchen world
Of exotic teas
And luxurious slivers of rich, dark chocolate.

Downstairs,
Clay-heavy days
Are left in the hall,
Mud on the soles
Of their lined-up shoes.

Transmuted,
By the consecration
Of curling incense,
The lowered light,
The room welcomes them
Into a seated circle
Around the altar
And the charm is done:
The room,
A sacred space.

Here,
They may sit with themselves
And each other,
Seen and heard,
In naked trust,
Stripped of the uniforms and masks.

Here,
They rediscover jewels
Scattered down the road
Of their pasts
And gently trace
The intricate, repeating patterns
Of their scars and sorrows.

Here,
They reach out ready hands
To help each other up,
Their aching knees
and hearts
Soothed.
It is a place of healing
And hope:

Melting

Carol Ward

Your soft fingers fall onto mine.
Melting snow, waxen thin.
I think of my bad hair days,
your beating heart,
those voices and visions
that crucify and perplex.
On a good day it's aripiprazole and citalopram,
regularly taken daily.
If I miss more than once, the voices will return no doubt,
then the promethazine to help me sleep,
and curtail those chattering demons,
that clothe me in a sack cloth of shame.
I want to build a snowman, will you join me?
I think you will be ashamed of my weakness, the
side effects of meds, that build my stress,
and when overloaded I snap but you,
more than anyone else understand,
You are the wax in an array of candlelight
that will not burn out.
I uncover my light and help others now.
do peer support and aid those who see and hear things too.
Keeps my heart beating and the dogs at bay.
The silver lining in a live forged from grit,
depression, psychosis and determination.
To heal the falling, by helping others, assisting myself too.
The snowman melts but we make another,
clearing winter pathways for better days.

Mosaic

Yvonne Ugarte

Do not ask me how I'm feeling.
Instead, talk to me about the weather,
your families and the R numbers.
I am happy that you are well and yes,
your garden looks lovely and I, too,
cannot believe the ineptitude of our Government,
the "not parties, but gatherings" that took place.
Yes, my family are keeping well
and lockdown has been tough for us all.
I am always happy to chat online or on the phone
but please do not ask me how I am.
I am not weak.
I am one of life's survivors
Yes, I have broad shoulders
so you can always lean on me
I would rather think of everything else
than stop and listen to the thoughts in my head,
spinning like ballerinas in clogs
But there is a smile on my face
Can you see it?

The mask slips.
I no longer know who I am.
This too will pass.
And a broken vase becomes a mosaic when put back together

Seek and Find

Jason N Smith

When plans go awry and ends don't quite meet
Find me between the cracks of hearts concrete
When feeling alone anchor and rudderless,
sister, father, brother, motherless,
Find me between percussions of heartbeats, I
That place where breath, death and living life meets
When your legs are laden and feet heavy as lead, I
Fearful of the hills and the valleys to tread
Amid your cordite clouds of battles last stands
In those desolate landscapes of no mans lands
Beyond every obscured word vision and sound
Find me in every single manifested blessing abound
And be found both shallow and profoundly complex
In extremes of emotional love to neglectfully vexed
And when you are rising again from your lowest of plights
Or dizzying in the highest of heights
Find me in the darkest of nights and lightest of lights
Where the veil is revealed renewing new sights
Gracing a light, a might, a purpose, love and release
When you finally surrender and find blessed peace.

I Am Both

Masha Bennett

I am both fading and I am blossoming
I am both vocal and I am mute
I am both passionate and "can't give a toss" -ing
I am both blunt and I am acute

I am both connected and disjointed
I am generous and greedy all at once
I am delighted and I am disappointed
I have a fluid and a rigid stance

I am full of anger and compassion
I am loving and indifferent - I'm both
I am logical and I am irrational
I work hard and I am full of sloth

I am fearless and I am oh so scared
I stand tall, and I am on my knees
I am defensive, and my soul is bared
I am both, and that is how it is

Escape

Colleen Cavell

Sometimes in the night…my heart starts to beat
in a crazy, tripping motion.
Stumbling like a child,
it dribbles out the beats in gooey gobs.
Congealing and then flowing
in a weirding, stop and start me, motion.
Filled with longing sighs…
and those low and desperate sobs.
Oh how often we get lost…
betwixt the dark and unknown wonder.
We gaze from curtained rooms,
behind ever-closing doors.
And we strip the senses bare…
just to push the dark asunder.
Whirling madly…gladly…sadly…
Falling feebly on all fours.
There's no sense or sensibility…
no hand upon a stalling heart.
Just a mind gazing out
towards the ever-receding stars.
To escape…break the bonds that bind…
Tear the flesh apart.
For the wonder of the free space…
and freedom of the bars.

Abnormal

Grace Fry-Rannila

crying and trembling
the sound of the forest in the rain
mountain peaks and plummets
indications of metamorphosis
it's all there in black and white
different shapes and new words
the lines and curves holding each other in intimate embrace
it seems so common
benign
just a neo-hieroglyph on paper
abnormal:
deviating from standard, typically undesirable
it has been following me from childhood into this minute
abnormal…
looking around normal seems disgusting
vile
normal is the death of
souls, societies, saints and sinners
normal is pop-up houses and cut-out cardboard people
the standard set by hollow monsters
unappealing
but the paper
it's waltzing, twirling giggles and squiggles
changed it all
now inside out
hanging me upside down
abnormal

was a badge of honor
a proclamation of valor
now a gun pointed at my head, cocked and ready
abnormal
the thick fog of uncertainty and dread
painting pictures of confusion and cognitive deterioration
fear soaking and saturating every cell in my body
reading
rereading
researching
reevaluating
revising
abnormal
to no longer be in control of me
lost in the world
the smell of shit and bleach
screams moans pleading
a possibility repeating itself like a scratched record
plastic tubes
water as thick as pudding
locked doors
those abnormal
contorting their faces into fake smiles
the hope for an end
a ceasefire of suffering
causing internal conflicts and sprouting guilt
"just wait until we find out how abnormal you are"
can't stop the terrors and the nightmares of wide eyes
abnormal
no awareness of present times
a living breathing memory
a prison of history
it's not death or god or no god or dark or fire

the threat is not in the possibilities of the end
madness and degeneration
years of senility
abnormal
the screaming pain of torture
hiding in shadows

Path Forlorn

John Thornton

the road to nowhere
abandoned dreams
they're ghosts of a past
or so they seemed

emotional thoughts
they come our way
for differing reasons
in the mind they stay

opaquely clearer
for a way ahead
looking behind
brings tears instead

time will move on
mended or torn
a cold wind blowing
on the path forlorn

Foggy Days and Hazy Pain

Matt Pugh

I wake up and stare at the meaningless numbers on my phor
Is it time to wake yet? Foggy day begins anew.
I drag clumps of sleep from needy eyes
and feel the hazy pain of yesteryear.
Kettle on, coffee needed to face the awaiting day.
Paint on a smile, breathe deeply, key in the door,
house locked tightly.

Travel to work, mind races with thoughts of nothing
I want to think on very long,
Foggy outside, foggier inside and the weather so drab
mirrors the grey of my soul.
As the train chugs to destination I try to settle and focus,
the constant train of thought moves faster
than this train taking me to work.
I arrive, I finally get my head in the game,
at last the flow of the river of torment in my head subsides,
my job provides sanctuary as I need
both grey cells to function here.

The day ends and the haze settles again,
like clockwork the mind kicks in right on cue,
A myriad of ideas, thoughts, worries and concerns,
I arrive home mentally fatigued, I sit at the piano and play.

The tune keeps time with my tears
as they drop from tired cheeks.
I run a bath, I sit and write to burn
the last of the fuel I have for the day.
I pull sheets over a busy mind,
the eyes close, the mind wide awake.
Then it comes again…..the alarm goes…..

Heebie Jeebie's

Peter Sanderson

Don't like dark stories
Don't like dark thoughts
Reminds me of you
and the problems you've got

Don't like the horrors
Don't like the creeps
Reminds me of you
when we've spoke with no sleep

Don't like the demons
Don't like the devil
Reminds me of you
Saying you're going to heaven

Don't like gargoyles
Don't like faces of clowns
Reminds me of you
when you're less up than down

Don't know why
I write at night
When it's the darkness

That gives me the shites
It's only for you
I face the fears that I do

That's when your thoughts
Give me the plots
The words and the rhymes
Have no vision of time
So in the dark
Long through the night
I'll stay where I am
Continue to write

It's only for you
I do what I do
Through all the dark clouds
The thundery nights
If not in my arms
You'll be kept in my sight
Protecting you, precious
With all of my might

I'm Going Through Something

Christine Smuniewski

I'm going through something
Something awful.
Something beautiful.
Something I some days have no words for
Sometimes I feel ecstatic
My emotions are through the roof
Then at the drop of a hat
I am down in the dumps
I'm going through something like ascension
I have all the symptoms
And then it takes a turn
And I feel like I've reached the end of the Earth
I'd like to crawl underneath a rock and hibernate
For a few years and not come back out
until I have this stuff figured out…
When "this too shall pass".
I'm going through something…

Compelled

Charlene Uma-Obong Efiong

The burning flame
Deep within
Ever consuming

Basking in blissful unawareness
Trapped in the recklessness of her life
Slowly withdrawing from reality

Too lost to realise the damage caused
She lies trapped in her beautiful cage
Needing nothing but the poisons she so
desperately craves

Her body a slave to the high gained
For without it she's wracked with need
A compelling desire she refuses to acknowledge

An ache deep within her that cannot be described
But if left unchecked could cause her demise

As We Were As Children

Maura Hogan

When we are young
We are open to everything
We are just beginning to find our limits

We are all unique and honorable
in the infinite variety of possibilities
we are all a miracle.

Yet as we age
There can be a funnelling
of our hopes and opportunities.
Or is it opportunities, then hopes.
This constricts our childlike acceptance
of a world that is kind and caring.

We have allowed loud men
to dominate a world meant for all.
But the pendulum is always in motion.
Help our world to be more kind and thoughtful
Help us to keep caring
And laughing
And growing
As we were as children.

But this time.
At the first sign of mean…..we name it.
And we expect better.

Together…..we can.

Magpie Moods

Elle Mort

The first was sorrow,
You bathed in her tears
Your unwanted companion
Throughout the years

The second one was joy
Her visits were brief
She arrived amidst laughter
Then left like a thief

The third was a girl
And was gentle as rain
She was kindness and knowledge
And healed all your pain

The fourth one, a boy
Was so wondrous to see
He was clothed in the sky
And ran wild and free

The fifth made of silver
Was wrapped round your wrist

Forged by the fire
From stardust and mist

The sixth one was gold
Mined from the land
Given in token
As your wedding band

The seventh was secret
To keep it was brave
You carried it with you
From cradle to grave

Lost or Missing Memories

Anne Buchanan-Brown

The Past slips its tether,
floating further from the jetty,
trailing the rope
that had secured it
to my present.

Decades elude me,
hiding in the woods
or leaving for kinder climates.
I hardly miss them.
A vague tension
in my forehead,
the red backs of my eyelids
concern me more right now.

Once,
the hours,
the days,
the years
the decades,
took things as they came.
There was no time for plans or memories,
just journeys
lurching back and forth
between disaster and respite,

now wiped clean,
to my relief,
from the account book
of cares
to be carried forward in the balance.

How else could I survive?

Fanciful Mysticism or Grounded Philosophy

Douglas Colston

"Shiva and Shakti,
some say,
are indistinguishable.
They are one.
They are the universe.
Shiva isn't masculine.
Shakti isn't feminine.
At the core of their mutual penetration,
the supreme consciousness opens".

Energy, ability, strength, effort, power and capability
and happiness, welfare, prosperity, bliss and liberation
are what they are
and integration of the two
(for those that see them
as distinguishable
[which need not be the case
at a fundamental level])
is typically associated
with union, harmony, setting things right and attention
[sam-adhi {'supreme consciousness'}]) -
there is no need
to attribute gender to them
or for that matter
to anthropomorphise the concepts…
each has adequate definitions
that are just (and) fine.

44

Yearning

Dorn Simon

Yearning, churning
Growling inside
Filled frustration
Gaping wide
Dire angst
Despair sank
Hollow centred
Open frank
Empty shell
Ridden well
Forlorn frown
Tarnished crown
Beats heard
No words
Noise loud
Silence bound
Broken heart found
Empty inner realms
Umbilical cord thrown
Emotions drown
Twin souls cross
Love to lost
Pain to fear
Yearning cheer
Braving being here
Kneading fragments
Cracking shields

Armoured up
Wielding heal
Live n learn
Build a home
Scream n shout
With without
Wrapped in arms
Come the calm
Lift release
Walk away
Left to fend another day
Ripped to shreds
Guts not head
Juxtaposed
Killing those
Darkest depths
Abysses wept
Rid this hell
Nurture quell
Love in light
Dark as night
Spirits within
I dispel

You Dice With the Devil

Gwen Taylor

You dice with death
You crossed a line
You veered from your side
Into mine
Then you left the beaten track
Crossed the bridge,
No way back
Into the water from over the side
Into the ocean deep and wide,
With me in the passenger seat
No escape,
Darting feet
Trying to swim my way back up
I realise that we've become tied up
Tied irreversibly together
Doomed to stay this way forever
I am tied up by your stick
Desperately I fight with it
Untangle myself
Climb on deck
The rope gets stuck
Around your neck
Then you sink
Down to the bottom
With the car right round your neck
On top of
Pinning you right down to the ocean floor

You can't take it
But I give you more
This is for the chides you wouldn't take
This is for the stick you used to shake
Why'd'you take control of me
I told you but you couldn't see
Why'd'you take the passenger side
The lines are clear, stay inside
We need to go back to the start
Where in wintertime we'd share a heart
Instead of so far apart
Forever, so far apart

Wallflower Life

Hahona Pita

In my quiet place
I could escape
my secret Elysium
sacred to a child of despair
a space to balance the ledger
yet I find my wherewithal fleeting.

Lost within the bounds of knowing
never quite grasping enlightenment
calloused hands no longer able to bear the strain
this horse has pulled up lame
I've blazed my last trail
campfire embers long since gone.

Tumbleweed thirst
no oasis on the horizon
dust permeates pores
no more leather and lace
just an empty vessel
but for a beating heart.

In my mind I've travelled to far away places
galaxies beyond the reckoning of sight
Argonauts sojourn of dreams

but I've fallen
voices call from the other side
behold…..
tables have turned.

I've said many a word in regret
accusations and silence
I can read your mind
your eyes give it all away
your stare vanquishes my manly gloats
I gave it my all
pushing through the carnage
but with every step I paid a toll.

I knew I couldn't stay
too many weeds to pull
no Garden of Eden
wallflower in disarray
I try to remember the good times
yet I cannot forge hope from decay.

I knew this day would come
when I had to say goodbye
I never meant to let anyone down
if only I'd turned the other way
just maybe I would have survived
but I was just a boy
and that demon killed me inside.

THE MELTING POT II

Just an innocent boy
and the pain is as fresh as wet paint
blood oozing sores
that boy never healed
yet though he grew to be a man
he was incarcerated in mental carnage
an ever-present trespasser
who never went away.

These once powerful limbs grow feeble
strength abandons me
the rot has set in
barely treading water
buoyancy abandons me.

I thank you for the gifts of love and life
but I am haunted,
endless darkness and torment
hate me if you must
but this soul is spent.

With a heavy heart
it's so sad to say goodbye
wallflower turned to dust
grass was never greener
I disappear into the mist
one day Jupiter will be in Mars
and when the stars align
just maybe
we will again be as one.

Uncle

Elmien Wolvaardt

A poem lurks beneath the surface of my mind
A whale shape bulges up
But the water doesn't break

You were the last
You knew my father's past
You have his calves and ankles, don't you know?
His closed-eye laugh and silver whiskers too

What did you see when you would dive beneath the blue?
The family were all so proud of you
A navy diver stronger than the rest
Not even cousin Colin could beat your best

With quiet twinkles in those naughty pale blue eyes
You kept your secrets close with little smiles
And barbecues in style

But nothing ever tasted as good
As my father in a happy mood

You knew him before he was sad

Before he was broken
before he turned bad

Was he good?
Was he kind?

Did you still love him or just get by
When he had to play daddy
And smacked you till you cried?

Your broken mother made him chief
Stole his childhood like a rotten thief

The army made him worse
A shouty sergeant major
with lips so thin and terse

Who barked orders at children
And when he wanted to impress
would demand a show
for special guests

Made us play and perform
ignorant of the storm
building inside of me

But over the whale-shape
The water bulges
It does not break

The whale turns
The water churns

And the ocean swallows it whole

Synthesiser

Carol Ward

If I were to describe my pain,
its synthetic and ethereal tendencies,
towards light, shade and colour,
I would draw a line somewhere between
each lobe and cortex.
I laugh when I think of the words
cerebellum and hippocampus.
Appears an apocalyptic minefield of neurosis.
A hippo belly of strange proportion.
Add environment, nature and nurture.
Makes me a somewhat peculiar creature.
Yet embrace these quirks, wear your brain as a crown.
They are like no others.
Not synthesised down.
Live your music and poetry even when the darkness spreads.
As it will unburden you from being alive yet dead.

Reflections

Teresa Bullock (Marcano)

I Value Me

End to the Era of Sadness
Washed away by a judge's pen
Washed away from my heart by the efforts within
Now on the path to who I was meant to be
I know my worth
I value me
It doesn't matter if the world can see
I know my worth

Dance

I took your hand and entered the dance
To brave what could be if given the chance
Your eyes were warm, but heart lies cold
The sorrows within remained untold
As our bodies swayed to the music played
The warmth glowed and the pain gave way
Two spirits blended, suspended in time
Connected in life by one thin line
A line that pierced your heart and mine
And bound our souls through space and time

Mistress

I agreed to the terms at the start
And know well the limitations this brings
You are but mine for a moment in time
The length of a long embrace
Your kiss remains warm on my neck
And lingers long after you've gone
I don't know why I stay in this place
But if I go, I must go alone

,

Shadows Only Cast in the Presence of Ligh

Ariuna Turi

I bitterly face,
in the crepuscular soul of my own race,
An ancient aptitude for disgrace.

The butterfly turned parasitic worm,
This maelstrom of malicious metamorphosis,
The idealised isolationism of catharsis,
The sinful silence proclaimed the arsis.

Heinous hyenas consume the decomposing corpse of God
Cackling at the sanctity of life,
Fate is unkind, the cutting blind knife.

Failing to have learned object permanence,
The fool feels not the urgency when sight is abstinent,
The superficiality grips and twists the perverted eyes,
Praising demons in gods disguise.

The primordial survival subconscious stirs subpar souls,
They seek imaginary wealth in a dying world,
Reduced to living day by day doing what they're told,
Values bought and sold,
They blindly wonder where comes the sorrow.

The scholar of bought and sponsored knowledge,
Speak of human nature,
Discarding the abstract reality of us as a legislature.

But shadows only cast in the presence of light,
One can't be dying if not otherwise alive,
No perverted eyes without the presence of sight,
No sorrow if not for knowing delight.

There's beauty in broken bridges,
Crooked paths that lead nowhere,
They teach you how to wonder,
To care not for life's blunders.

My Internal World

Trudy Annie

Survival strategies,
of a traumatic childhood, unfurled,
life changes, impearled,
influenced by the environment
and people making me disturbed,
gaining peace and stability
living in this world,
holding back when feeling impulsive;
opportunities to rest much deserved.

Having so many confusing aspects
of my condition,
my internal world
will always be part of my life,
that's been affirmed
by me, and by them.

My behaviour and emotions
change any crisis -
or concerns for my safety -
I can be referred back,
specialist help was needed,
the way people treated me
has been undeserved.

I am a caring, wonderful person,
that has truly been scourged.

Will They Remember Us?

Gae Stenson

When we are gone will they mourn us,
remember us.
Will they recall us at all,
Will they deny and just forget?
We, who withdrew from this world
Now seeking the assurance
Of knowing
We'll be a loss to someone or maybe a regret.

When we are gone and the world continues on,
Will they grieve us?
Those who deceived us, who ignored our plea
For justice and integrity,
Will they finally validate our fight
Acknowledge our plight, or continue with their slight
Never recognise our pain in word and deed,
Will we just recede
Into the tragedy of our own history.

Renew

Anne Buchanan-Brown

Today, I know that nothing can destroy
The peace that is the still place
In the centre of my cracked heart.
I know the stuff that stuffs the cracks
Is strong enough
to stop my light from leaking out.

The lives of others touch me still,
But only brush me with a gentle hand;
I do not need to bear their pain,
I do not need to know or understand.

Each day now washes me in its soft sight
And I can rise without carrying the burden
Of the darkness of the moonless, vanished night;
I set it down, renew, and walk into new day's light.

I Give Up

Dorn Simon

They say it's easy to give up
That it's a cop-out
Cowardly
I disagree wholeheartedly
The mind-bending struggle it takes
For a decision of any kind to make
To view all angles and those within
To recognise your life's yet to begin
Subsisted through circumstance alone
Teased or hinted at some wee throne
To have all hope held off fast
As absolutely nothing ever lasts
Faces of supposed friends
Loved ones at worlds end
Society increasingly toxic
Repetitive wars the subject
Non child-bearing loner
Blessed by chance with another's
Though not mine to grasp
They too will go fast
Not a leg to stand on see
This in essence how will always be
One can find some motivation
Infuse ideas with activation
Dream of where want life to go
Yet deep down always know
A shell, lifeless with agonising core

Feel as though always wanting more
Yet what is here is easily lost
I have nothing for the life at cost
Tired from holding up these shields
All and any efforts not yield
Coming up to Fifty-Five
It's obvious I shouldn't be alive
I lived once, a happy life
OK yeah was filled with strife
But somehow a carefree nature did exist
Then great changes caused amiss
From moving, shifting betwixt
Some toxicity surfaced
From holding self up even as child
My coping mechanism was going wild
I have honestly tried everything
To be of goodness in society
I even did 26 years of sobriety
I wish to aid in healing world events
At least aid those suffering lament
To offer a space of understanding and care
Yet external reactions deemed unfair
I no longer know who sees straight
Is it me or they at Hell's gate
I am worn and torn all used up
Each time I loved came at a cost
My life was over many moons past
The life God gave somehow lost
Whether I am or not a toxic mess
I no longer know I must confess
I give up as no step can take
Cannot do right for doing wrong my namesake
At least I can ascertain I am no fake

But a life of purpose I cannot make!
This all sounds so self-absorbed
Even my poetry full of distort
I lay waste to a person's life
This space on earth I fill disliked
On the contrary life is precious
Earth as a whole filled with fascination and beauty
Good people exist though somehow few
If I am one of them I have no clue
I give up being uncertain
I give up hiding broken behind this curtain
I give up being target of abuse
I give up querying my own misuse
Do I incite or invite this crass
Am I a sociopathic mess?
Diagnosed not yet others point
Perpetual merry-go-round of disjoint
I give up spending my each waking hour
Deliberating who is the enemy in this shower
Shower of broken debris
Is it them or is it me?

Acceptance

John Highton

Nobody cares locked inside their head
You keep trying you listen to what's been said
Two times please God may the third be a charm
'Cause the vipers in my head will always cause more harm
The truth of the self the only one that matters
And I'm looking at you all seeing blood splatters
'Cause I'm sick of chasing other people's dreams
Trying to help while I fall apart at the seams
'Cause I'm something people try to manipulate
To meet their own ends and now I truly hate
The way that I am the more that I try
The more this world makes me want to cry
To scream my rage and say back the fuck up
I've finally looked in the mirror at what the demons took
Surrounded by sycophants people with eyes
Hearts and minds full of deception and lies
Sometimes their own sometimes implanted
By people who forced and just ranted
Look at your life is it really that bad
The things I've seen and experienced I should be that sad
And yeah I've tried to kill myself let myself go
So here it is let me let you all know
My first memory watching my Mum's neck breaking
Second one the same person atop my Mum raping
Alcohol drugs I can still hear the screaming
The love I wanted I was always just dreaming

The older I got I tried to stand too
When you look at me you all thought you knew
Think I wanted this by choice or design
All thinking I'm crazy like I've lost my mind
Little boy trying to fight a grown man
And you all thought I wanted to, like I have a plan
Everyone says you're just like him God damn
And you all thought I was a dreamer chasing dreams
And I was the dreams of others so it seems
But I'm still here stood like ancient stones
And just 'cause my life's always been the battle zone
Don't think I'm defeated 'cause the world tried
I'm only who I am because of this ride
So Aurora awakens another day got my first clue
They can't put me down too strong from what I've been through

One More Step

Catherine Campbell

I'm standing at the precipice,
undaunted by its edge -
precisely where I need to be,
to carry out my pledge.

I'm standing at the precipice,
my heart outside my chest -
pulsing strong, triumphantly,
in honour of my quest.

I'm standing at the precipice,
with courage heaven sent -
fears unburdened by the path,
to honour my intent.

I'm standing at the precipice,
my spirit set to soar -
life has walked me here today,
in search of something more.

I'm standing at the precipice,
alive in every sense –

Not Alone in Despair

Susan ILA Davis

I wish for you connection
Safe place where you can sleep
Afraid for real affection.
My dear this makes me weep.
Who will become your consort
Will you be wrapped in arms?
Or will wings come to transport?
To keep your heart from harm.
A worry for a stranger
There's sadness on your brow.
The miles away from comfort.
Hope you find light somehow.
Your words flow a sad release.
Reach eyes of those who care.
I witness their words of peace.
We relate but can't repair

Love, Joy and Delight

Paul Wilkins

Your mind and emotion hold the key
They're the things that set you free
Whate'er the day
Whate'er the night
Fulfil yourself with love, joy and delight

Sadness and worry
Gets you nowhere at all
Just up the wall
Whate'er the day
Whate'er the night
Fulfil yourself with love, joy and delight

With faith in the Lord
And determination
You may live a long and happy life
Whate'er the day
Whate'er the night
Fulfil yourself with love, joy and delight

Let people come first where'er you go
That's a thought
All people should know

Whate'er the day
Whate'er the night
Fulfil yourself with love, joy and delight

Love, joy and delight
Love, joy and delight

Inner Realms Exhumed

Naema Sinclair

Ah, the dream unravels and dissolves before my eyes
Like snowflakes melting in sultry desolation.
In a not too unfamiliar pattern
We know the rules of this game
Melt, dissolve
Open to the next adventure.
Same sweet desire,
Open, Open, absorb and transmute.
I would not absorb they blows
Nor return thy smite.
The snares of this world,
Though tawdry and bright are but demons
Who swallow the flowers.
Dine out on your ineptitude.
Let it fill out the belly of your hollowed out soul,
scratch another notch on your pubic belt.
But leave me the fuck alone.

Demolition

Philippa Waters

My home is a reflection of myself;
a shrine to neglect
and despair.

Cracked, cluttered, chaotic.
Its wiring faulty
and dangerous.

Incapable of rebuilding itself.
Not caring enough
to even try.

Stepping Out

Sarah Jane Hull

I used to step out of myself
And watch myself from afar.
Sometimes from the sideways
Or lurking in the back
The best was when I floated.
Hovered just above.
Although I never talked of it
I came to realise
Not everyone has this gift.
Not everyone can fly.
Internally
I made a rope
So I don't just float away.
I'm now a lot more normal
And don't fly everyday.
I choose to be more present
I decided for myself
I now know much more clearly
It was my mental health.

Tainted

Charlene Uma-Obong Efiong

She sits and stares at the waves
Hoping without hope for inspiration
nd tries not to let her mind fill with thoughts of forlorn caves
And people screaming in trepidation

She revels in the feel of her toes in the sand
And breathes in the warm air
While staring blankly at the pen in hand
As the wind dances with her hair

Yet nothing but the darkened thoughts and crying skies
Thoughts that the child should not bear
She stares at the sea, hoping to find solace
in the often-told lies
For the mother does not care

She tries to ignore the footsteps approaching
Hoping they'd go away
She tried to ignore the figure encroaching
While watching the fronds sway

She doesn't want him here
Tainting what she thought untaintable
His footsteps invoke fear
Making her unable

She closes her eyes and slowly fades
Her eyes open, the eyes are hers, but not
Enjoying the feel of the west-going trades
A smile curves on her face as she recognises the arrogant t

Her eyes move to the pen in hand
The figure now behind her
Her thoughts unplanned
He meets his reaper

The Grey Mist

Amita Sarjit Ahluwalia

Let no one come to disturb the grey mist
(But they will)

So many stories.

They fell in love and now she is dead
There's a picture of her smiling

There was a green tree field space in the plains
Where the five well-dressed people stood smiling
It seemed like a photo taken at a wedding

The white flower in her dark flowing hair
gave her a Hawaiian look
She leaned smiling on his confident back

Will you fetch my coffin and bury me
beside my parents, she asked,
He promised but died first himself

To not cry she tried to make a Zoom link
to the funeral service

Eat your food. she said.
I don't care, he said.
You'll turn weak, she said.
I don't care, he said.

Join Facebook. No, it's fun.
OK. No harm trying.

Let's build that lobby on the first floor.
Add a lift.
I can't climb the stairs.

The daughter was a dancer and the son a lawyer.
Both wore white shirts.

The coffee is too weak.
I don't like too much sugar.

Census? The Municipal Supervisor?
No, his daughters, one married, the other still studying.

So many houses are locked.
There's a cold wave.

How many geckos died of the cold?
How many birds?
Or dogs or cats or cows?
Or mosquitos?

Death is all around us. So is life.

Any time now, the bell will ring.
Bury yourself in the bedclothes.
Escape, escape.
The rag seller calls.
Life will not be denied.

Stories come knocking.

Find it and lose yourself in it, the grey mist.
(They will, they will).

The MIND Boggles

(at the time, out of patience, exasperated)

Stuart Watkins

When dealing with MIND,
You hope you will find,
A sympathetic ear,
A message that's clear,
Some welcoming hugs,
Not vandals, or thugs.

I reached out to MIND,
I was lagging behind,
I wasn't to know,
I'd find a shit-show.
I thought they'd be kind,
Not an absent-MIND.

Poetry's my thing,
Because I can't sing.
I asked folks to write,
It was met with delight.
Poems galore,
Flew through my door.

THE MELTING POT II

I'd started a club -
But from MIND, just a snub.
No inclusion from them,
Just silence and phlegm.
My efforts ignored,
As if they were bored.

A charity, kind hearts?
No! Faeces and farts.
The blurb I had penned,
Reached an untimely end,
They couldn't be arsed,
Though I'd shared my bleak past.

My poor mental health
Was consigned to a shelf,
My project of sharing
Brought out their uncaring,
We're so busy at MIND
That we're deaf, dumb and blind.

I wrote many times;
I wrote many rhymes;
I gave them ten chances,
Ten wordy advances;
They weren't met with violence,
Just nothing. Just silence.

I don't trust in MIND.
I think they're unkind.
I don't think they care,
I don't think they're there.
Their bad attitude,
So disgustingly rude.

So if I were the boss,
I'd root out the dross,
Kick them to the kerb;
I'd write a new blurb.
They'd be forced to be kind.
I'd be changing my MIND.

The Negative Us

Sunil Sharma

Our negative feelings
And thoughts are
The chemical reactions
In our minds
And the arguments are
The chain reactions
That lead to
Quarrels among friends
Fights in the streets
And wars among nations

The anger and hatred
Spread fast like venom
The rationale and logic
Evaporate
Leaving our mind a devil
That hits the harmony
And peace
To lead terror, atrocities
And abuse

Sometimes
these chain reactions bring
Insane destruction and misery
That humanity may later

Be ashamed and regret
But those accountable
Are rarely punished
War that brings
Unnecessary grief to the innocent
Is the greatest crime on earth

The Fragile Flame

Ariuna Turi

The failing flame flayed on the tortured torch,
Yet it still scared shadows spurring from sinners' souls,
They found in each other kindred kindling,
Without each other not whole.

The opposites danced through eternity,
Finding fraternity in their taciturnity,
As the sharpest blades,
They held the prerogative of fragility.

Away from God's grace,
In a monotony of disgrace,
They watched as sparks turned to life,
As steps of man replace voids embrace.

Hiding from animalistic artists,
Cryptic caves hide under the mountains' gaze,
Attempting horrible reality to paraphrase,
While setting the void ablaze.

There was born poetry,
The fragile flame that extinguishes the winter,
The shadow that the whole world enclosed,

THE MELTING POT II

There in the line of neither light nor dark
lies the first rhyme composed.

There's an underground causality,
that holds together all of reality,
That has somehow forgotten man in its creation,
Are we but agglomeration of pointless animation?

Maybe we are the larvae turned butterfly,
For consuming the corpse of God,
Trimming our own roots,
For the fake beauty of the bonsai.

In the centre of every dead star,
Lies the grimoire of the scar,
Fate's failed Avatar.

And the poet awakes under lightless chandeliers,
Immune to the moon's phases,
Not comprehending the evil incongruences of those phrases
Listening to the ominous owls,
Unconcerned with fate's predatorial prowls,

We looked at the space between every star,
Waiting not for the sun,
But for the day he would not understand but become.

Painfully Shy

Rose Drew

She knows she is too thin,
feels bruises form on her protruding hips
just leaning against the liquor shelf
silent
watching them drink;
but she can't stop yet.

One night her weight becomes
a topic of discussion
among the drinkers hiding out
in the ancient dusty pub:
"My DEAR", smirks Gay Bob,
"It's not even VICTORIAN!"

Still she leans, silent,
tongue-tied shyness,
gratefully invisible;
slipping out from shadows
to refill a glass,
drag up a case of long-necks
from the damp dungeon basement,
strong despite thinness:
scooping off the dregs
of wasting muscle.

Still they discuss her,
turning bleary interest outward,
so safer than in -
even she can agree.
But she can't stop yet.
Not until she's lost enough weight.
Not until she completely disappears.

Emotional Revolution

Catherine Campbell

Today, I cradled Sadness,
I met her in the eye.
"I'm leaving you", I whispered,
And urged her not to cry.

She fought with her displacement,
Afraid of letting go.
"I need the space", I told her,
"For happiness to grow".

Today I held my Anger,
I gazed upon her face.
"You're fear disguised", I whispered,
"Deserving of more grace".

She felt resistance melting,
Her circuitry rewired,
"I'm leaving you", I told her,
"So love can come inside".

Today I hugged Forgiveness,
I held her hand in mine.

"I've searched for you", I whispered,
"You found me just in time".

She coursed throughout my bloodstream,
Dissolving all my pain,
"You've rescued me", I told her,
"Now peace can take her reign".

Today I kissed Elation,
Alluded I was free…
Asked if she might contemplate
A walk through life, with me.

She didn't need to answer,
I saw it in her face.
"Yes my love", she whispered,
"I've longed for your embrace".

The Attack

Jo Broderick

My heart bled that day
The day I saw you lifeless on the ground
I was shattered completely
Before you came around
My soul screamed out for yours
As I watched you bleeding on the floor
And as you came around
I could barely recognise you any more
You are the man I love
Your face and body torn asunder
I could not control myself
When I saw one man, my soul turned to thunder

This day I had the capacity to kill
To take the life of someone else
Just as someone had tried to extinguish my love
The fact a year on it's still awaiting a trial
This is making me ill
I saw the video, it should have gone viral
But instead my partner and I are left to spiral
Is this really what you call justice
I call this disgrace

You have the pictures of his face
You have the videos taken on CCTV
You have his clothes for DNA heavens please
At this point you're protecting his aggressors

Far more than aiding the victim
And this just measures up to a hell of a broken system

I didn't lose the love of my life
He recovered physically anyway
But mentally the scars persist they won't go away
He gets angry when I talk about this night
He gets infuriated he didn't have a chance to fight

Knocked out from behind a very cowardly move
Afraid you couldn't face him, damn right you're being sued
I hope you rot for turning my life upside down
I hope you can't sleep, I hope you can only frown
You did this to us don't even ask us for forgiveness
You certainly won't get it from me
You won't get it from us
I don't even know you but I despise the air you breathe
I can't stand that it's the same air as me
I hate any time you feel free
Plead guilty, and I hope they throw away the key
My partner has not been the same since you did this
He used to love life, we would always kiss

He used to love going out
His music was what he was about
He had to relearn every damn thing he knows
Just because your fun night was out of control
He finds it hard to work out that which he loved before
The night I saw him lifeless on the floor

Bohemian Dreams

Hahona Pita

Earth mama
Papatuanuku
I just killed this man
having lived an empty life
letting darkness rob my light
I'd given up the ghost
given up the fraughtful night
choices made in times of pain
I pulled the trigger without fright
but mama…
I never knew…
I was just a wayward soul
a hurt boy within a man's shell
no stars upon my sky
no light upon my day
but mama…
what is life?
is it really worth the strife?
when darkness became my light
and tears offered no respite
I'd given up the fight
but mama…
I never knew another way
ghosts haunted me anyway
I'd walked upon your shores
but I was just
a washed-out salty soul

103

I needed carriage
in your embrace,
Papatuanuku…
I threw it all away
and today I said farewell.

Killing Time

Robert Phillips

Fear and loathing
Go hand in hand
Confidence drifts away
Like grains of sand
Making mistakes
Again and again
Routine failure
Is such a pain

Always wishing
For something more
How did my life become
Such a chore
No one sees
The jester's tears
His insecurities
And his fears
Behind the laughter
Fun and comic turns
The agony of life
It still burns

Life is not a rehearsal
We only get one shot
Wasting time

Even one minute
Even one hour
Compounds the crime
Make every day
Special
remove Trivial things
Aim for the blessings
That this life brings

Hate casts a long shadow
It will eat at your soul
Never let you rest
Till you lose all control
So set your sights high
Aim for the light
Bathe in the daytime
Turn away from the night

Stitch

Fin Hall

Some days it's hard to face the reality
that the world goes on outside your door,
While you struggle to get out of bed and stumble,
fumble to the kitchen and pour yourself a cup of ambition.
The contrition in your head and the condition
that led you to the place you are now,
where indecision is first choice
and the small voice inside your head gets louder.
The recurring thought prevails that you are stuck
between going off or staying on the rails
just waiting to see what train comes first.
Another day, another dollar, the silence becomes a holler,
uncertainty and confusion, is your life just an illusion?
Getting hard to sort out truth from fact. Ambiguous and failing,
you watch as the last ship is sailing,
leaving the safety of the harbour: leaving you behind.
Your mind in constant turmoil hardly knowing what is up,
always feeling lowly, feeling down.
No matter how you attempt to alter, your attitude still falters,
causing oscillation and dilemma,
hoping the line is not already crossed.
It's OK to not be OK, it's OK to seek out help.
There are those who will offer you a hand.
Be aware that all is not lost, you don't have to pay the cost
there are ways to help you to get through.
So when all is said and done, you know you're not alone.
There are people out there who care.

Protecting

Peter Sanderson

I may be a picture of strength
A torso that looks so bold
Inside there's a weakness
A fear of getting old
It's only when I hold you
My power starts to unfold
It's the want and need to protect you
To love, to have and to hold
That is when I forget
One day I will be getting old

Watching Out for Rabbit Holes

Sarah Jane Hull

I fell down a rabbit hole.
I fell beneath the floor.
I laid there trapped
And lost
And couldn't find a door.
There was no white rabbit
To help me out.
No grinning Cheshire cat.
The only way I survived
Was to breathe
And dig
Until I saw the light.
Now I'm much more wary
Of Rabbits
Moles
And Bats.
I step a bit more lightly
Scanning all the time.
Avoiding those
Rabbit holes
That seem to fill my mind.
Now I've got a shovel
And I play
Whack-a-mole.
Sending all those Rabbits
Back down their horrid hole.

Futuristic Visions

Christine Smuniewski

He thought he was just
An average Joe
But no
He was much more
He belonged to a higher source
And he received spiritual downloads
Some moved him
Some brought him to his knees
And when they did
He knew his God was
Surely something interesting
And he always questioned
Why it was he
Who had to receive
These visions
He wanted to know
Why it was to him
They were given
Sometimes he didn't
Want to have these
Futuristic visions
But his God
Had a plan
And a purpose.

Mental

Susan ILA Davis

I can't compete in deficiencies
I learned that from the start.
Sometimes it forms from environment.
We are not far apart.

It might be passed from birth to you.
Chemical imbalance?
They classify as a disorder.
Something we should challenge.

Cause of schizophrenia unknown.
Psychotic episodes.
Could medications now overthrow?
Precious drugs, heaven knows.

Manic - Bipolar and many more.
The costs are really high.
They still have so much more to explore.
Don't want lost ones to die.

Glimmers

Maura Hogan

Help…..I feel a crisis coming on.
The signs are there.
The anxiety rising, the med schedule disrupted.
What will I do.
You see it's my offspring, my loved one.
Out there.
Trying to live their life.
Finding hardship daily. Her struggle is within.
I have watched it evolve.

The parent challenge: what to express, and how.
The fear is real.
Family history.

Previous attempts. Self harm.
Thoughts, feelings and emotions of the most vile sort.
All I know is to love.
Love and being patient.
Because our lives are in our own hands.
Such a quandary.
With optimism at the end of my story.
Because there is always hope. And glimmers.
And get-togethers. And Christmas and New Years.
And the idea that we can all heal from wherever we are.

Angels v Demons

Carol Ward

When it's angels versus demons
in this game of mental health roulette.
We keep a bright light burning,
the dragon makes an erstwhile bet.

St. George did strike the dragon out,
though there are serpents in this land.
Who are tools of our cruel system,
won't lend a helping hand.

When playing good cop, bad cop,
they do not get the score.
That love is what is lacking,
what we are asking for.

Brushed with a dove's kind feathers.
Sailing against the wind.
It's angels versus demons,
we wonder who will win.

With love, grace and honour,
is the battlecry ahead.
The spirit of love please prevail,
joy and wonder met.

Eyes Meet

Isabelle P Byrne

She would talk to me through the mirror
I thought it pretty weird,
Until I realised it was her attempt for eye contact to disappe

She'd avoid my eyes as if she'd be caught,
Knowing that intimacy wasn't something she'd been taugh

So she shudders when I meet them as if she'd been pinne
Her face of horror as she thinks I see her sins,

A relentless game of cat and mouse,
A girl stuck within her own jail house,

Safe behind the rusted bars she had made her home,
A life living with the dead in the depths of the catacomb

But every time we meet her eyes begin to shift,
Her smile begins to grow and the darkness starts to shif

She's safe now here with me,
She opened the jail house door and let herself free.

Just Another Lost Soul

Laura Mochan

The bleak city streets so dark, so grim.
My lonely soul alone, its light too dim.
Chaos and carnage, hearts are broken
But the words are rarely ever spoken.
The neon night's busy, empty and full;
Shattered my heart, crushed my skull
With its never ending poison and noise,
I remember that I am not here by choice.
Father's at work, mother's probably pissed.
I know with certainty that I am not missed.
Not thought of, and selfish, a screw up, yes.
A disappointment, embarrassment, just a mess.
I'd say sorry, I would, but for what I don't know.
To be safe, to be loved, and not on my own
In this place of putrefied stenches and fear,
Where strangers come close; come far too near.
This cold is too cruel, invading me, killing me.
To die or to steal, again; I'm forever debating
With myself as I fight to retain who is me;
Who I am, what I'm made of, who I want to be.
I am lost roaming free, but a prisoner in mind,
While I try to find somewhere to leave me behind.
Not here, in this hell hole, in this neon abyss,
I want to return to find myself enveloped in bliss
Where birds fill green trees and their song is sweet,
Warm and inviting, a million miles from the streets.

A dream so embracing that I have every night
Where I'm happy and needed and not out of sight.
In it I'm at home, safe, warm and I'm wanted.
All the little I need, without question, is granted.
I'd say sorry, I would, but for what I don't know.
But I cannot go back, I just cannot let this show,
All this darkness and hate that lives deep inside.
I must stay as I am, I must fight, I must hide.
They'll forget me soon, but I'll always know,
That they have created just another lost soul.

Rinse and Repeat

Chris Husband

I wanted to
I really did
But my inner power
Fell off the grid
I couldn't walk
I couldn't talk
My motivation up in smoke
This grey and heavy malaise
This cloudy gaze
This whirling, swirling, unfurling daze
Close my eyes
Take the fall
And hope that I feel nothing at all

Mr and Mrs TV Personality

Jason N Smith

The guy on the street corner,
scraggly beard, messed up hair,
shoes hanging off his feet, takes
a walk down the street.

People are looking at him,
people are moving away,
got no time for this stray man
they would rather pass,
than give passage into their homes.

They'd rather pass over cash to the shops
than the man looking at them,
saying, please help me.

The scraggly-haired man on the streets,
The one people pass marching their feet
and they do not want to meet,

scraggly-haired man, unkempt, rejected,
but this scraggly-haired man is a brother,
a mother's son,
this scraggly-haired man is someone,

THE MELTING POT II

See he did not always dwell on the streets,
he could have been your Alan Sugar,
your Branson, your Richard Pryor,
he could have been your brother,
but you smother your eyes and walk on by,
moving your feet to different destinations,
passing the scraggly-haired man,
scraggly beard that you feel an alienation from,
but this scraggly-haired man is more than you have become,
because he is reality,
and you are a materialistic commercial seen on TV.

Give me a smile,
big teeth,
pout your lips,
paint your eyebrows,
shine your shoes, but
this scraggly-haired man,
he's got respect, because
this man is not rejected by the world,
only rejected by you,
Mr and Mrs TV personality.

Love and Hope

Charlene Ima-Obong Efiong

The crunching of dry leaves beneath her feet
Drowned out by her joyful giggles
The autumnal colours
Seemingly calming her restless mind

She dances round the garden
Calling out the names of the flowers
All the while the mother watches
A wistful smile on her face

She sees as her daughter
Lost in her own world
Unknown to the pain caused
Dances round the garden

For her daughter, she has only love
She cares not for the whispers often heard
Or the pitiful looks never concealed
She cares just for her daughter, lost in a world of her own

Shopping Blues

Jane Badrock

I can feel the tears coming as I walk down the aisle.
A young woman stacking tins gives me a caring smile.
"Can I help you?" She asks, as she gets to her feet.
If only she knew. But she's young, unspoiled and sweet.
A wave of emotion makes me unsteady. I sway.
I sigh deeply as I feel my pain ebbing away.
"Im OK", I reply, and at last there's no guile.
The moment has passed. I'm back. And I pay back her smile.

Legend

Anne Buchanan-Brown

Under the railway arch,
The ruin of a former legend snores.
Flakes of dulled metallic dandruff,
Scatter like confetti,
Loosened by the idle scratch
Of filthy, unclipped claws.

His puny wings
Twitch in his dream
Of long-lost flight,
Failing to spread full-span.

His hoard of dragon gold is spent -
Squandered
On some ageing maiden's
Over-ripe delights.
Empty cans of Special Brew
Tell their own tale;
His brandied breath
Has set the place alight
Just once too often
For his timid landlord's tastes.

Needless to say,
She got the cave,
The kids,
The cache….
She'd said that it was only right….

And so,
Tonight,
A legend,
Once a dragon,
Snores under the railway arch
Lost in a dream
Of endless flight.

Post-Natal

Carol Ward

You sit among shells,
Darling buds, May days,

under her bosom a baby grows.
Another woman yearns.
Did God say no?

Leaves her barren and spurned,
then out of the blue, a chime of wedding bells.

She took him for a clown,
this man about town.
Gave her what they needed
and so they breeded.

She bore a son and to this day.
They don't know why they took him away.
A band of social workers, clucking mothers,
drove her apart from the son and lover.

Yet today she remains, not jealous of her sister's fortune,
but oozes pain.
Post-natal depression is no gift.
A mental stigma that never lifts.

Now there are perinatal units, more help for new mothers.
Yet still she misses her son and lover.

Every single day.
Only writing takes
that grief away.

Zopiclone Trip (Melting Pot III)

Stuart Watkins

Drop the Zop.
Tastes like metal. A rush of GABA….
Will not spit out….help me sleep, help me sleep

Heroes have tried to enter,
but the walls are made of stone.
The tower was made before Time began,
from the mightiest stone.
Heathen warriors hammer and batter,
but their weapons are powerless.

The treasures within are not for a barbarian's eyes.
Entrance forever denied,
an impregnable fortress to mortal beings.

The way in….

dissolve into particles,
very molecules of thought,
spread into mistcloud,
move *through* the stone,
through the stone.

It is welcoming. It beckons, invites, accepts.
Drawing in,
magnetic, pulling upward,
a staircase, a skyward, spiralling coil,
drift in, drift up,
drift in, drift up.
Climb above the sky, above the stars,
float….rise….float….rise….

A chamber, a cavernous hall, songs….
Musical truths, mathematical truths,
philosophical truths, spiritual truths.
My being….all beings….
My form….my face….
changing, moving, melting, merging.

Woman, man, child, spirit,
fish, bird, tree,
lion, tiger, wolf, bear,
wind, rain, river, desert, mountain, forest.
Thunder, lightning, hurricane's eye.
Natural power, unnatural power, all power.

A female smile of safety, a vision of pure love and calm,
crying, smiling, showing, teaching,
shining, sharing, caring,
protecting, embracing, loving.

Wisdom. Faith. Hope.

TRUTH.

The purest love,
sun, moon, ocean, sky, star,
all as one, all radiance, all unified energy,
all space, all time, all merged,
all have become one entity,
pure consciousness, all consciousness,
one essence,
bathe in the essence,
join with the essence,
become the essence.

I am the essence, formless and disembodied,
spirit and matter,
ether and plasma,
bathe in the essence,
surrender to the essence,
be the essence,
feel the essence,
everything is the essence,
here, now, never, nowhere,
everywhere.
bathe in the essence,
universal essence.

Bathe.
Bathe.
Bathe.

128

Love Poem

Anne Buchanan-Brown

I flay my heart, bare of skin,
It barely keeps the life-blood in.
I give my soul, they call it sin,
For this is where the dark begins.
I sink into a sightless grin,
I feel it crawl across my skin,
And then I let the demons in,
That steal my soul and name my sin
And then the nightmares all begin,
While you look on and grin and grin.

Watching Seasons

Jason N Smith

(A poem written from behind walls)

I try, I tried and am trying again
For happiness to flow from my pen,
I try to disregard bars and close walls
And find the beauty in snowfalls,
each snowflake is never the same,
holes in white blanket with patter of rain,
Snowdrifts, banks, children squealing on sledges,
everyone safe with no unseen ledges;
but no, I tried, it does not work,
darkening shadow seems destined to lurk;
just how do I forget freedom-less-ness?
And the fact I created this mess?

How about spring which is so filled with hope,
springs springing and gathering down a slope,
threading valleys and meadows awakening blooms
where cottage shutters are open airing out rooms;
shutters bring to mind my solitary….
Locked in a room with no stimuli, not any;
and a surreal madness melting one's mind,
making even the nastiest person conversing seem kind.

Summer comes with a high pollen count
bumble bees, wasps, but of flowers, no amount.
If only flowers could grow through the stone,
I would pick one for my cell-like home.

In many prisons the autumn has lots of clout,
Come the rain and prisoners never let out,
but when I am lucky leaves blow over the wall
and apart from beautiful nature, this signals the fall.
Around full circle another winter has come,
but not a good time when moods follow sun;

But I try, and am trying again
for happiness to flow from the pen.

To the Stars and Beyond

Janet Tai

Tonight, you are here
Flashing brilliance across a cloudless blustery night
Through the swaying of the trees,
I see all of you - twinkling! twinkling!

If there were higher powers humanely possessed
I'd pluck you down one by one
Contain you to set aglow
The dark confines of my dreary room;

You'd tell me stories of the constellations
Of your eight friends
Alkaid, Mizar, Alcor, Alioth, Megrez, Phecda, Merak, Dubhe
They who structured the Ursa Major - The Great Bear
Or better yet
Dazzle me with tales of the vast galaxies
The Milky Way and Andromeda;

If I could have you for an hour
Or even a moment
If I could morph into you
Everytime you come out to play

Anything is better than here
Earth,
Life,
Living!!!

Printed in Great Britain
by Amazon